Words of
COMFORT

Words of
COMFORT

Copyright © 2006
Brownlow Publishing Company
6309 Airport Freeway
Fort Worth, Texas 76117

Scripture quotations are taken from the
following versions:

Holy Bible, New International Version (NIV).
Copyright ©1973, 1978, 1984
International Bible Society.

The King James Version of the Bible (KJV).
Used by permission.

ISBN 1-59177-234-6

Printed in Singapore

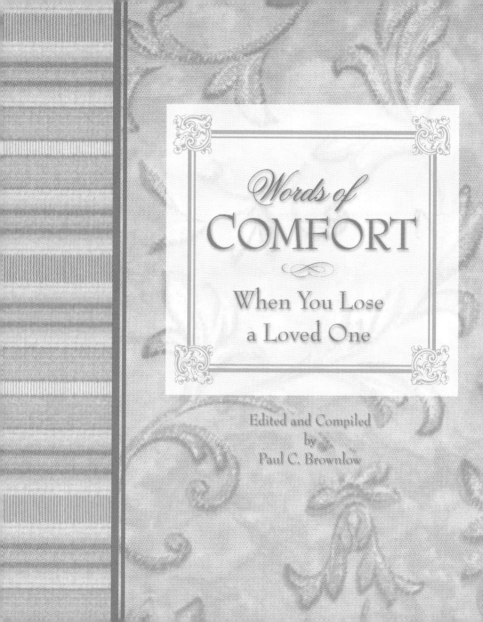

Words of
COMFORT

When You Lose a Loved One

Edited and Compiled
by
Paul C. Brownlow

In My Father's House

❦

In triumphant faith we live in the soothing solace
that only a part of us shall ever die. The Bible says:

For we know that, if our earthly house of this
tabernacle were dissolved, we have a building of God,
a house not made with hands, eternal in the heavens.
(2 Corinthians 5:1)

❦

In speaking of another house designed
to last forever, our Lord once said:

Let not your heart be troubled (sorrowful but not
troubled): you believe in God, believe also in me.
In my Father's house are many mansions: if it were
not so, I would have told you. I go to prepare a place
for you (it is a reality). And if I go and prepare a
place for you, I will come again, and receive you unto
myself, that where I am, there you may be also.
(John 14:1-3)

❦

Another Room

No, not cold beneath the grasses,
Not close-walled within the tomb;
Rather, in our Father's mansion,
Living in another room.

Shall I doubt my Father's mercy?
Shall I think of death as doom,
Or the stepping o'er the threshold
To a bigger, brighter room?

Shall I blame my Father's wisdom?
Shall I sit enswathed in gloom,
When I know my loves are happy-
Waiting, in another room?

Robert Freeman

When we get to Heaven,
God will not look over us for medals,
degrees or diplomas but for *scars*.

Hubbard

❧

Be strong and take heart
all of you who hope in the Lord.

Psalm 31:24

❧

Be not afraid in misfortune. When God
causes a tree to be hewn down, He takes care that
His birds can nestle on another.

❧

The *Lord gives* His blessing
when He finds the vessel *empty*.

Thomas á Kempis

God Knows

I know not, but God knows;
Oh, blessed rest from fear!
All my unfolding days
To Him are plain and clear.

I cannot, but God can;
Oh, balm for all my care!
The burden that I drop,
His hand will lift and bear.

Though eagle pinions tire,
I walk where once I ran;
This is my strength to know:
I cannot, but God can.

Annie Johnson Flint

Where There Is No Sorrow

This earth is a land of smiles and tears, and as we pass through it we are visited with both. It is comforting, therefore, to know that our beloved has ended this pilgrimage where joy often turns to sorrow. Having completed the journey, our loved one has moved over there where:

God shall wipe away all tears; and there shall be no more death, neither sorrow, not crying, neither shall there be any more pain; for the former things are passed away. (Revelation 21:4)

Leroy Brownlow

No Eye Has Seen

No eye has seen,

no ear has heard,

no mind has conceived

what God has prepared for

those who love Him –

but God has revealed it

to us by His spirit.

1 Corinthians 2:9, 10

The Secret of Life and Death

In eight short words, the Apostle Paul revealed
for all time the secret of life and death:

To live is Christ,

To die is gain.

Philippians 1:21

When we understand the true meaning
of life and its purpose, we will not fear death—
it will bring our reward.

While we should not be afraid of death,
we must also not be afraid to live.

Jesus did not come to explain
away suffering or remove it.
He came to fill it with His presence.

Paul Claudel

*The greatest tragedy of life is
to have no burden to carry.*

Unknown Fourth-Century Preacher

Surely God is my salvation;
I will trust and not be afraid.

Isaiah 12:2

*As sure as ever God puts His children in the furnace,
He will be in the furnace with them.*

Charles H. Spurgeon

*Hope is the power of being cheerful
in circumstances which we know to be desperate.*
G.K. Chesterton

❧

God has revealed many truths
which He has not explained.
We will just have to be content to
let Him know some things we
do not and take Him at His word.
B.A. Copass

❧

**So much has been given to me, I have no time
to ponder over that which has been denied.**
Helen Keller

❧

With everlasting kindness
I will have compassion on you,
says the Lord your Redeemer.
Isaiah 54:8

We Trust in Thee

O God, help us to trust in Thee
at all times, and never to doubt
Thy promises and love. In our duties,
grant us Thy help; in our dangers,
Thy protections; in our difficulties,
Thy guidance; and in our sorrow,
Thy peace.
May Thy grace be sufficient for us,
and Thy strength made perfect in
our weakness; and bring us at last to
Thine eternal kingdom, through
Jesus Christ our Lord. Amen.

Unknown

Now We Understand

When we lose a loved one, we
finally come to understand truths
that before were only words:

-There are things worse than death.

-Learn to hold loosely all that
is not eternal.

-The earth and all therein is but
a passing pageant.

The Lord your God is with you,

He is mighty to save.

He will take great delight in you;

He will quiet you with His love;

He will rejoice over you with singing.

Zephaniah 3:17

~

There are times when God asks nothing
of His children except silence, patience and tears.

Charles Seymour Robinson

~

*The only ultimate disaster that can befall
us is to feel ourselves at home on this earth.*

Malcolm Muggeridge

~

Hope dries the tears on the cheek of woe.

John MacDuff

The Shepherd Psalm

The Lord is my shepherd; I shall not want.
He maketh me to lie down in green pastures:
He leadeth me beside the still waters.

He restoreth my soul:
He leadeth me in the paths of
righteousness for his name's sake.

Yea, though I walk through the valley
of the shadow of death,
I will fear no evil; for thou art with me:
Thy rod and thy staff, they comfort me.

Thou preparest a table before
me in the presence of mine enemies:
Thou anointest my head with oil;
My cup runneth over.

Surely goodness and mercy shall follow me
all the days of my life:
And I will dwell in the house of the Lord forever.

Psalm 23

The Lord Is My Shepherd

It was David, the ancient shepherd boy, who poetically
and pictorially expressed the hope of frail humanity
in the eloquent and immortal Twenty-third Psalm.
For hundreds of years, on every shore and in every
clime, it has dried the tears and healed the hearts of
countless numbers who helplessly stood by and watched
as husband or wife, son or daughter, father or mother,
brother or sister slipped down through the valley of
the shadow of death. Its words have been upon the
trembling lips of millions who slowly turned from the
flower-decked mound where the earthly frame they
loved so dearly was placed to rest in hallowed ground.
And later, when time stood still in mournful shadows,
as they tried to put back together a broken heart, they
found peace in the way of life and death provided by the
Good Shepherd. Today our needs are no different.
And the Shepherd's Psalm is still a balm for hearts
that ache and bleed and break.

Picture ourselves in the Middle East. The sun is
radiant-hot. The earth is scorched dry. We see a few
wobbly sheep nibbling at burnt grass already bitten too

close to disappointing ground. Sheep without food, without water, without future.

But wait! There is more to the picture. Our view broadens, and standing by we see the shepherd. His existence is as real as the sheep. And his presence, power and providence change the entire outlook. In complete trust, David proclaimed, "The Lord is my shepherd. I shall not want."

The shepherd has information not possessed by the sheep. Their knowledge is so limited. But he knows beyond the hills there is a valley where life is pleasant.

The shepherd calls and the struggling sheep, in an effort to follow, muster the last full measure of devotion and the last fading ounce of strength. They know not where they are going, but they know the shepherd. That is enough. They trust him. Each has the assurance: "I shall not want."

The journey commences. Clouds of dust form and hang over them in choking discomfort. There are rocks to avoid lest famished sheep stumble never to arise. There are holes to bypass; otherwise spindling legs may be mortally entrapped. There are thorns stretching out to cut and tear; so a detour is in order. But on they go laboriously wending their way down the hill, adjusting themselves to the conditions along the trail. At last they arrive in the valley of plenty. The shepherd has supplied their needs. The sheep who had nothing without him now have everything with him.

They "lie down in green pastures beside still waters." They eat and are satisfied. They drink without fear, for the shepherd has led them away from the rushing, roaring current to where the water is still. There is quiet without and peace within.

The shepherd has restored them. He has led them in the paths of goodness for his name's sake.

But don't think there have been no dangers or ordeals. However, in spite of both, they feared no evil. Life without fear! And for one reason and for one reason only — the presence of the shepherd! That made the difference. That was the source of their security.

So David, once a shepherd, used this soothing imagery to describe his own relationship to his own Shepherd and to account for his own life without fear. His confidence in the Shepherd of all shepherds gave him a gallantry marked and made famous by this heroic declaration: "I will fear no evil: for thou art with me." That's why "thou art with me."

Fear has been replaced with comfort. "Thy rod and thy staff they comfort me." Comfort! One of man's most crying needs and David found it - not through his own power, but through the power of the Good Shepherd.

The lowly sheep are favored with a prepared table. "Thou preparest a table before me in the presence of mine enemies." Wild animals encircle them. They growl and howl, but keep their distance.

They dare not come any closer or they shall have to fight the shepherd. The sheep enjoy protection because they have a protector; and this makes life good, though there are enemies.

Now the day is far spent. At last comes the night. And as the evening shadows lengthen, the shepherd manifests more mercy. He has provided a fold or an enclosure, and at the door he stands and personally greets all who enter. He anoints every head with oil and quenches every thirst with a cup of cold water, brim-full and running over, as extra benefactions.

Then the door of the fold is barred. The sheep are as safe in the night as in the day. They sleep in peace. Assurance is their fortune and hope is their benediction.

David sums up the hymn of praise with a powerful poetic declaration: "Surely goodness and mercy shall follow me all the days of my life: and I will dwell in the house of the Lord forever."

Forever! There is no end. What we call the end is only transition –just a new beginning.

Leroy Brownlow

God Will Help

Build a little fence of trust
around today;
Fill the space with loving work,
and therein stay;
Look not through the sheltering bars
upon tomorrow;
God will help thee bear what comes
of joy or sorrow.

Mary Frances Butts

God had one Son on earth without sin,
but never one without suffering.
St. Augustine

❧❧

The Lord is my light and my salvation—
whom shall I fear?
The Lord is the stronghold of my life—
of whom shall I be afraid?
Psalm 27:1

❧❧

Teach us, O Lord, the disciplines of **patience**,
for to **wait** is often harder than to **work**.
Peter Marshall

❧❧

Cast your cares on the Lord and he will sustain you;
He will never let the righteous fall.

Psalm 55:22

Fortunate are the people whose roots are deep.

Agnes Meyer

God washes the eyes by tears until they can behold
the invisible land where tears shall come no more.

Henry Ward Beecher

The truest end of life is to know
that life that never ends.

William Penn

What then shall we say?
If God is for us, who can be against us?

Romans 8:31

Give You Peace

The Lord bless you and keep you;

the Lord make his face shine upon you

and be gracious to you;

the Lord turn his face toward you

and give you peace.

Numbers 6:24-26

With God

So on I go, not knowing;
I would not, if I might.
I would rather sail in the dark with God
Than sail alone in the light.
I would rather sail with Him by faith,
Than sail alone by sight.

Mary G. Brainard

In Glory

What must it be to step on shore,
and find it – Heaven;
To take hold of a hand,
and find it – God's hand;
To breathe a new air,
and find it – Celestial air;
To feel invigorated,
and find it – Immortality;
To sail from the care
and turmoil of earth
To one unbroken calm;
To land there and find it – Glory.

The Waiting Father

God is easily celebrated on the mountain tops of life.
But sometimes when we are on the mountain,
we build altars to ourselves and turn our backs on
the One who brought us there.

Whether we celebrate Him on the mountain or not,
God is better known and discovered in the valley.

When we are desperate, when we have no place else
to go or turn, when life is turned upside down,
God is there.

He waits to be needed. And when we come,
broken and bruised, saddened and in despair –
our God is there. He is the waiting Father.

Unfailing Love

Let the morning bring me word

of Your unfailing love,

for I have put my trust in You.

Psalm 143:8

Please, Lord

Please, Lord, teach us
to laugh again;
but God, don't ever let us
forget that we cried.

Bill Wilson

Our Grief to Destroy

Think not thou canst sigh a sigh
And thy Maker is not by;
Think not thou canst weep a tear
And thy Maker is not near.
O! He gives to us His joy
That our grief He may destroy.

William Blake

More Than Conquerors

In all these things we are more than
conquerors through him who loved us.
For I am convinced that neither death
nor life, neither angels nor demons,
neither the present nor the future,
nor any powers, neither height nor depth,
nor anything else in all creation,
will be able to separate us from the love
of God that is in Christ Jesus our Lord.

Romans 8:37-39

When we empty ourselves,
God Almighty rushes in.

A.W. Tozer

I will walk among you and be your God,
and you will be my people.
Leviticus 26:12

Everything has its wonders,
even darkness and silence.
Helen Keller

No one truly knows *happiness*
who has not *suffered*.
Henri Frederic Amiel

When He Carried Us

The Lord lifts us up when we have fallen –
and carries us when we are weak.
Anonymous

❧

He tends his flock like a shepherd:
He gathers the lambs in his arms and
carries them close to his heart.

Isaiah 40:11

The Beauty of Peace

Drop thy still dews of quietness,

Till all our strivings cease;

Take from our souls the strain and stress,

And let our ordered lives confess,

The beauty of thy peace.

John Greenleaf Whittier

Precious in His Sight

Death was appointed to emancipate us;
give us freedom from a world of sin and sorrow,
rebellion and regret. This liberation – death –
is one of the most precious blessings of God.
"Precious in the sight of the Lord is the death of his saints"
(Psalm 116:15). Death is not the blighting curse
that some have supposed, but a blessed necessity
made possible by the love and wisdom of God.

After God created Adam and Eve he placed them
in the Garden of Eden and enjoined a law upon them,
which they transgressed. Sin dwelt in the land.
There was the downfall of the human family.
It would not be in humanity's good interest to live
forever in a state of lawlessness, rebellion and
transgression. Something had to be done to liberate us
from such a state. So mercy was extended to our first
parents by our Father's driving them out of the garden
lest they "take also of the tree of life, and eat, and live
forever" (Genesis 3:22). Separation from the
tree of life brought death.

In our world as we know it, death is an essential
requirement of life. Suppose no living thing should
ever die. Suppose that in the animal kingdom,
animals are born and multiply and never die. Suppose
that in plant life, plants live and multiply, but not one
ever dies. Suppose that in the human family, people
live and continue to live, multiply and continue to
multiply, but no one ever tastes of death.
We see that life would soon become unbearable.

Death is a prerequisite of life. What a friend we have
in death – all our afflictions lose their hold. Suppose
the aged could only become older, the distressed
could only suffer more agony and the suffering could
only hurt more intensely – and no one could die.
There would be no future in this. Then living would
be a thousand times worse than dying; for the believer's
death is loss only to those who linger behind. For
those who remain on this side of the chasm of time, death is
loss, but for those who have crossed over it is gain.

Leroy Brownlow

Look to the Rainbow

Trust God where you
cannot trace him.
Do not try to penetrate
the cloud he brings over you;
rather look to the rainbow
that is on it.
The mystery is God's;
the promise is yours.

John Macduff

If sorrow makes us shed tears,
faith in the promises of God
makes us dry them.
Augustine

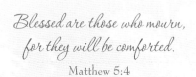

Blessed are those who mourn,
for they will be comforted.

Matthew 5:4

When it is dark enough, we will see the stars.

Ralph Waldo Emerson

I thank thee, O Lord, that thou hast so set eternity
within my heart that no earthly thing
can ever satisfy me wholly.

John Baillie

To Not Lose Heart

Therefore we do not lose heart.
Though outwardly we are wasting away,
yet inwardly we are being renewed
day by day.
For our light and momentary troubles
are achieving for us an eternal glory
that far outweighs them all.
So we fix our eyes not on what is seen,
but on what is unseen.
For what is seen is temporary but
what is unseen is eternal.

2 Corinthians 4:16-18

The Promised Land always lies

on the other side of a wilderness.

Havelock Ellis

They Live On

God calls our loved ones,
But we lose not wholly
What He hath given;
They live on earth
In thought and deed
As truly as in His heaven.

John Greenleaf Whittier

Believe Not a Word

Someday you will read in the papers that
D.L. Moody of East Northfield is dead.
Don't you believe a word of it. At that moment
I shall be more alive than now. I shall have gone
up higher, that is all - out of this old clay tenement
into a house that is immortal; a body that death
cannot touch, that sin cannot taint, a body
fashioned like unto His glorious body. That which
is born of the flesh may die. That which is
born of the spirit will live forever.

D.L. Moody

A Little Bit of Heaven

There is something majestic about seeing old men
and women who wear the crown of many winters
on their heads. In their faces are etched the joys
and sorrows of the world. They have fought valiantly
for honor and virtue and purity and righteousness.
And by their efforts, they have helped to bring
a little bit of heaven to earth.

Their hands are weathered and wrinkled from helping
the young, the weak, the widows and fatherless,
those who couldn't find their way, the lost. They have an
inner peace about them that quietly permeates
their life and all those around them. It is our honor
to have known and loved them.
It is their glory when they get to go home.

Greater Than Gold

For a little while you may have had to suffer grief

in all kinds of trials. These have come

so that your faith – of greater worth than gold,

which perishes even though refined by fire –

may be proved genuine and may result in praise,

glory and honor when Jesus Christ is revealed.

1 Peter 1:6-7

Every experience God gives us,
every person He puts into our lives,
is the perfect preparation
for the future that only He can see.

Corrie Ten Boom

*The Lord gives strength to His people;
the Lord blesses His people with peace.*

Psalm 29:11

I believe there is nothing that honors
God more, or that God more honors,
than praising Him in tribulation.

Brownlow North

*God takes life's pieces and
gives us unbroken peace.*

W.D. Gough

He Longs to Be Gracious

Yes, the Lord longs to be gracious to you;
He rises to show you compassion.
For the Lord is a God of justice.
Blessed are all who wait for him!

Isaiah 30:18

Beautiful Beyond Belief

These things are beautiful beyond belief:

The pleasant weakness that comes after pain;

The radiant greenness that comes after rain;

The deepened faith that follows after grief;

And the awakening to love again.